TODAY'S ★★ ARMY ★★★★ HEROES

by Joyce Markovics

Consultant: Fred Pushies
U.S. SOF Adviser

BEARPORT PUBLISHING

New York, New York

Credits

Cover and Title Page, © Leif Skoogfors/Corbis, © Shane A. Cuomo/CNP/Corbis, and © U.S. Army/Sgt. Travis Zielinski, 1st ACB, 1st Cav. Div. Public Affairs; 4, © Spencer Platt/Getty Images; 5, © Ramzi Haidar/AFP/Getty Images; 6T, © U.S. Army; 6B, © Scott Nelson/Getty Images; 7, © U.S. Army/Patrick Albright; 8, © David Furst/AFP/Getty Images; 9T, © AP Photo/Charles Dharapak; 9B, © Pat Vasquez-Cunningham/Albuquerque Journal/ZUMA Press/Newscom; 10T, © U.S. Army; 10B, © AP Photo/David Guttenfelder; 11, © Reuters/Landov; 12, © U.S. Army/Spc. Anita VanderMolen; 13, © Mandel Ngan/AFP/Getty Images; 14T, © AP Photo/U.S. Army; 14B, © John D. McHugh/AFP/Getty Images; 15, © U.S. Army/Personal photo of Staff Sgt. Robert Miller; 16, © U.S. Army/Personal photo of Staff Sgt. Robert Miller; 17, © AP Photo/Pablo Martinez Monsivais; 18T, © AP Photo/U.S. Army/Spc. Micah E. Clare; 18B, © U.S. Army/82nd Airborne; 19L, © Paul Avallone/ZUMA Press/Newscom; 19R, © Shamil Zhumatov/Reuters/Landov; 20, © J.D. Whitmire; 21, © AP Photo/U.S. Army/Sgt. Jim Wilt; 22T, Courtesy Sergeant Jason Mike; 22B, © Radu Sigheti/Reuters / Landov; 23, © Courtesy Sergeant Jason Mike; 24T, © U.S. Army/Sgt. Jonathan W. Thomas; 24B, © Bob Strong/Reuters /Landov; 25L, © U.S. Army/Sgt. Jonathan W. Thomas; 25R, © Michael Reynolds/EPA/Landov; 26, © Simon Lim/ Pictobank/ABACAPRESS/MCT/Newscom; 27, © Andrew A. Nelles/ZUMA Press/Newscom; 28, © Torsten Blackwood/ AFP/Getty Images; 29T, © R. Corner/Shutterstock; 29B, © U.S. Army/Mr. Michael William Petersen (SDDC); 31, © Keith McIntyre/Shutterstock.

Publisher: Kenn Goin
Senior Editor: Lisa Wiseman
Creative Director: Spencer Brinker
Design: Dawn Beard Creative
Photo Researcher: Picture Perfect Professionals, LLC

Library of Congress Cataloging-in-Publication Data

Markovics, Joyce L.
  Today's Army heroes / by Joyce Markovics ; consultant, Fred Pushies.
     p. cm. — (Acts of courage)
  Includes bibliographical references and index.
  Audience: Ages 7 to 12.
  ISBN-13: 978-1-61772-445-9 (library binding)
  ISBN-10: 1-61772-445-9 (library binding)
  1. Soldiers—United States—Biography—Juvenile literature. 2. United States. Army—Biography—Juvenile literature. 3. Courage—Juvenile literature. 4. Heroes—Juvenile literature. 5. Combat—Juvenile literature. I. Pushies, Fred J., 1952– II. Title.
  U52.M37 2012
  355.0092'273—dc23
                              2011036125

For more information, write to Bearport Publishing Company, Inc., 45 West 21st Street, Suite 3B, New York, New York 10010. Printed in the United States of America in North Mankato, Minnesota.

10 9 8 7 6 5 4 3 2

★ ★ ★ Contents ★ ★ ★

Fighting Two Wars 4

Grenade Attack. 6

Honoring a Hero 8

Ambushed! 10

One Against Two 12

Unthinkable Bravery 14

The Ultimate Sacrifice 16

A Medic's Mission 18

First Aid 20

Quick Thinking. 22

Fighting Through the Pain 24

A Job Like No Other 26

More Army Heroes. 28

Glossary. 30

Bibliography. 31

Read More 31

Learn More Online. 31

Index 32

About the Author. 32

Fighting Two Wars

On September 11, 2001, members of a **terrorist group** from Afghanistan **hijacked** four U.S. airplanes full of passengers. The terrorists flew two of the planes into the twin towers of New York's World Trade Center. They flew another plane into the **Pentagon**, and one plane crashed into a field in Pennsylvania. In all, nearly 3,000 people were killed.

The twin towers after being attacked on September 11, 2001

The terrorist group responsible for the attacks on September 11, 2001, is called **Al Qaeda**. Osama bin Laden was the leader of the group when the attacks were planned.

In October 2001, the United States sent troops to Afghanistan to destroy the camps where these terrorists had been trained. Then, in March 2003, the war on terror expanded into Iraq. Some U.S. officials believed that Iraq's ruler, Saddam Hussein, was building powerful weapons, including **nuclear** ones, to use against the United States and its **allies**. Though these weapons were never found, the United States, with help from other countries, was able to remove Hussein from power.

Thousands of brave U.S. Army soldiers served in Afghanistan and Iraq in the years following the September 11 attacks. This book recounts some of their amazing acts of courage as they faced terrible danger in service to their country.

The red parts of this map show where some of the events in this book took place.

TURKEY

Caspian Sea

TURKMENISTAN

SYRIA

KUNAR PROVINCE

AFGHANISTAN

Korengal Valley

Baghdad
Iskandariyah

IRAN

PAKTIA PROVINCE

KANDAHAR PROVINCE

IRAQ

PAKISTAN

INDIA

Persian Gulf

Arabian Sea

Arctic Ocean

ASIA

NORTH AMERICA

EUROPE

Atlantic Ocean

AFRICA

Pacific Ocean

Pacific Ocean

SOUTH AMERICA

Indian Ocean

AUSTRALIA

N
W E
S

Southern Ocean

ANTARCTICA

U.S. Army soldiers in Iraq in 2003

Grenade Attack

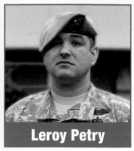

Leroy Petry

Rank: Staff Sergeant (Later promoted to Sergeant First Class)

Hometown: Santa Fe, New Mexico

Conflict: War in Afghanistan

Date: May 26, 2008

Honor: Medal of Honor

Army Ranger Sergeant (Sgt.) First Class Leroy Petry will never forget May 26, 2008. That's the day he led a team of soldiers on a **raid** to capture terrorists in Paktia **province**, Afghanistan. It was daytime when helicopters carrying the men touched down in a dusty village. Shortly after they landed, Sgt. Petry and a few of the others went looking for the enemy fighters in a building. Once they were inside the courtyard of the building, bullets suddenly started flying at them. They were under enemy fire!

Two U.S. Army soldiers looking for enemy fighters in Afghanistan

Carrying out a **mission** during the daytime is very dangerous, because it's hard to hide from the enemy in the daylight. Most missions take place at night, because soldiers can more easily hide in the dark.

Almost immediately, Sgt. Petry was shot in both legs. Then, without warning, an enemy **grenade** exploded nearby, wounding two other soldiers. Minutes later, a second grenade landed a few feet away from Sgt. Petry and the injured men. Despite his serious injuries, Sgt. Petry did the unthinkable. Without hesitation, he lunged for the grenade before it could explode. "I grabbed it with my hand, and I threw it as hard as I could," he said.

An Army soldier gets ready to throw a grenade during a training exercise.

Honoring a Hero

Even though Sgt. Petry acted quickly, he was not quick enough. When he opened his hand to release the grenade, it exploded. It ripped off his right hand, and tiny pieces of hot metal pierced his body. "I had never seen someone hurt so bad," remembered one of the soldiers who had been part of the same raid. Despite his life-threatening injuries, Sgt. Petry was able to bandage his hand and radio for help while still under enemy fire.

Like Sgt. Petry, U.S. soldiers in Afghanistan and Iraq use radios to call for help.

After the soldiers defeated the enemy fighters, one of Sgt. Petry's teammates rushed up to him and shook his left hand. "That was the first time I shook the hand of someone who I consider to be a true American hero," this soldier said later. Sgt. Daniel Higgins, another Army Ranger who was there that day, said, "If not for Staff Sergeant Petry's actions, we would have been seriously wounded or killed."

Sgt. Petry, a father of four, has a new **prosthetic** hand, which functions like a real hand. He can once again shake hands with others, and he has even learned to play golf using his new hand.

The Medal of Honor

President Barack Obama awarded the Medal of Honor to Leroy Petry, who was just 28 years old when he was injured in Afghanistan, during a White House ceremony on July 12, 2011. The medal is the U.S. military's highest award for bravery.

Ambushed!

Salvatore Giunta

Rank:	Specialist (Later promoted to Staff Sergeant)
Hometown:	Hiawatha, Iowa
Conflict:	War in Afghanistan
Date:	October 25, 2007
Honor:	Medal of Honor

Sgt. Petry is the second living soldier who received the Medal of Honor after serving in Afghanistan. The first was Army Specialist (Spc.) Salvatore Giunta. On October 25, 2007, Spc. Giunta and his **platoon** were in the Korengal Valley—one of the most dangerous places in Afghanistan. Moonlight guided them as they walked single file over the steep, rocky **terrain**.

The Korengal Valley in eastern Afghanistan has been called the "valley of death," because more than 40 American soldiers died there between 2006 and 2009.

Suddenly, shots rang out. **Taliban** fighters had **ambushed** the team. "There were more bullets in the air than stars in the sky," remembered Spc. Giunta. Luckily, he was able to seek cover. However, three of the men walking ahead of him were struck by bullets and seriously wounded. One of them was Sgt. Joshua Brennan, Spc. Giunta's close friend.

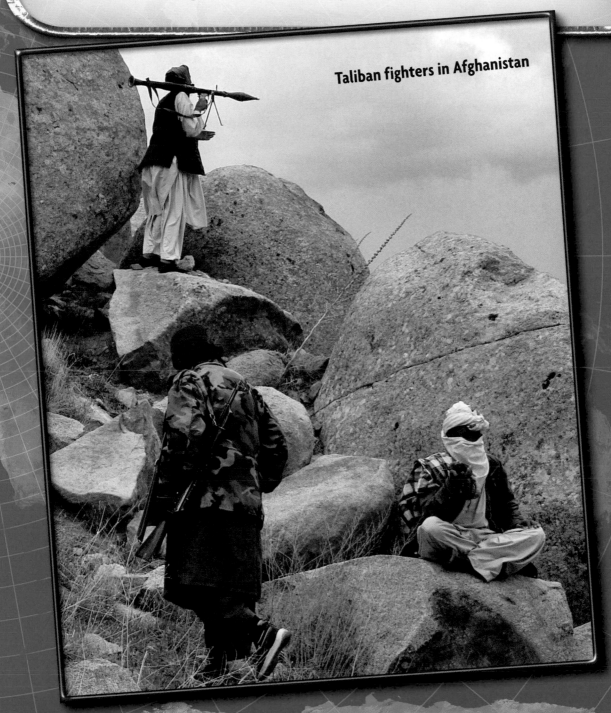

Taliban fighters in Afghanistan

One Against Two

Without hesitation, Spc. Giunta ran into a wall of enemy fire to drag one of the soldiers to safety. While doing so, Spc. Giunta was shot in the chest. Fortunately, his **body armor** saved him. With no time to waste, Spc. Giunta rejoined his platoon and began moving toward the two other injured men. He fired nonstop and hurled grenades at the enemy fighters. Finally, he and the others reached one of the men and rescued him.

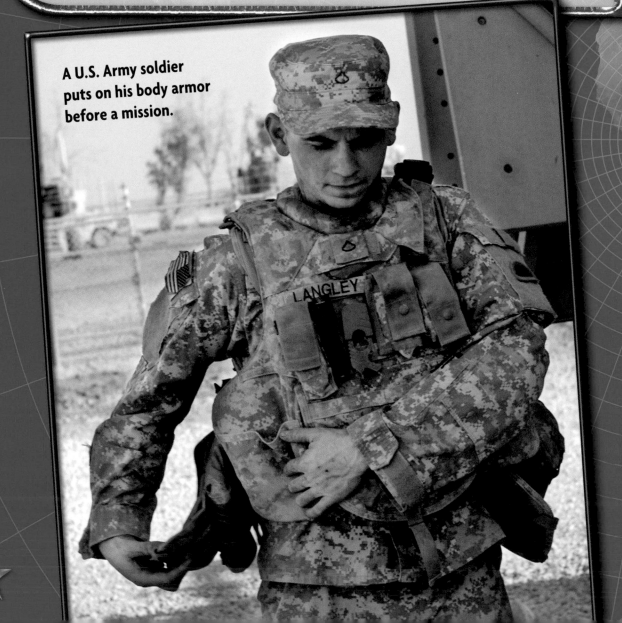

A U.S. Army soldier puts on his body armor before a mission.

Then, without concern for his own safety, Spc. Giunta ran ahead of his platoon to look for Sgt. Brennan. There in the darkness he was shocked to see two **insurgents** carrying away his injured friend. With a burst of energy, Spc. Giunta sprang forward and fired his gun. He hit one of the insurgents, who immediately fell to the ground. The other one was injured and ran away. At last, Spc. Giunta rescued Sgt. Brennan.

After Spc. Giunta dragged Sgt. Brennan to safety, he tended to the injured soldier's many gunshot wounds. Unfortunately, Sgt. Brennan died from his injuries the next day.

Salvatore Giunta received the Medal of Honor on November 16, 2010, during a ceremony at the White House in Washington, D.C.

Unthinkable Bravery

Robert J. Miller

Rank:	Staff Sergeant
Hometown:	Wheaton, Illinois
Conflict:	War in Afghanistan
Date:	January 25, 2008
Honor:	Medal of Honor

Like Sgts. Leroy Petry and Salvatore Giunta, Army Staff Sgt. Robert J. Miller also received the Medal of Honor—but not before he lost his life. On January 25, 2008, Sgt. Miller and his **unit** of about 20 men were in snowy northeast Afghanistan near a remote village in the Kunar province. They were on a mission to clear the area of insurgents. Sgt. Miller was leading his team down a narrow, icy trail when they were attacked by enemy fighters.

It can be very hard to get around on the rugged terrain of Afghanistan in the snow.

First one insurgent leaped out from behind a large rock, shooting at the soldiers. Then close to 150 insurgents started shooting from only a few feet away. The Army soldiers fired back. Dust and smoke filled the air. Sgt. Miller instructed his team to **retreat**. Then he did the unthinkable. Sgt. Miller moved in the opposite direction of his team—straight toward enemy fire. Why? So the enemy would fire at him and not at his team.

Sgt. Miller (center) with some Afghan soldiers

The United States is at war with members of the Taliban and Al Qaeda—not with the Afghan people. In fact, Sgt. Miller helped train some local Afghans to become soldiers to help the United States fight the insurgents.

The Ultimate Sacrifice

To protect his men, Sgt. Miller fired shots and threw grenades at the enemy fighters. He also used his radio to report the insurgents' positions to his team. During the battle, Sgt. Miller was hit twice in the chest. Still, he kept fighting and radioing his men to give them information about the enemy.

Sgt. Miller was just 24 years old during the battle in Kunar province.

When he was not on the **front lines**, Sgt. Miller loved the landscape of Afghanistan and sharing tea and conversation with the local people. He learned how to speak the Afghan language, called Pashto, to communicate with them.

Eventually, Sgt. Miller's radio fell silent. His unit knew that he had been killed trying to save them. Two fellow soldiers ran through the storm of bullets to be by his side. In all, Sgt. Miller saved the lives of more than 20 soldiers. "I would not be alive today if not for his ultimate **sacrifice**," said one of his teammates.

Sgt. Robert J. Miller's Medal of Honor was presented to his parents, Maureen and Phil, on October 6, 2010, at a White House ceremony.

A Medic's Mission

Monica Brown

Rank: Private (Later promoted to Sergeant)
Hometown: Lake Jackson, Texas
Conflict: War in Afghanistan
Date: April 25, 2007
Honor: Silver Star

Some Army soldiers, like Private (Pvt.) Monica Brown, have special medical training. As an Army **medic**, she treats wounded soldiers. On April 25, 2007, Pvt. Brown's skills were put to the test.

Pvt. Brown with a young Afghan boy in a military hospital

While traveling in a **convoy** in Paktia province, Afghanistan, one of the Humvees behind Pvt. Brown's vehicle hit a bomb called an improvised explosive device (IED). "There was a ball of fire that went into the truck and burned all five crew members," remembered Sgt. Major Michael Greene, who was also at the scene. After the bomb exploded, hidden enemy fighters started shooting at the convoy. Without hesitation, Pvt. Brown grabbed her nearly 50-pound (23-kg) first aid kit and leaped out of her vehicle into intense enemy fire to help the wounded soldiers. "I thought about every guy in that truck. 'Are they okay? I need to get to them now,'" recalled Pvt. Brown.

A Humvee is a large jeep-like vehicle that can travel up to 65 miles per hour (105 kph).

Pvt. Brown was on her way back to the **base** when the explosion occurred. Under U.S. law, female soldiers are not allowed to fight in Army **combat** units. However, they have other important jobs, such as working as Army medics or helicopter pilots.

IEDs are homemade bombs used by insurgents to attack American soldiers. Almost anything can be turned into an IED, including a garage door opener, a cell phone, or an old pipe, by adding explosive material to it.

First Aid

Pvt. Brown soon reached the Humvee. "Everyone was already out of the burning vehicle," remembered Pvt. Brown. "But even before I got there, I could tell that two of them were injured very seriously." She immediately used her body to shield the two critically wounded men from flying **shrapnel** and bullets. "There was pretty heavy incoming fire," said Pvt. Brown.

Pvt. Brown performs first aid on a victim who is pretending to be hurt during a training exercise.

Then, while still under fire, she and two other soldiers dragged the injured men to a safer area. Soon a truck arrived. Pvt. Brown and the other soldiers lifted the injured men into the truck and it sped off to a more secure location, just one mile (1.6 m) away. Once there, Pvt. Brown treated and prepped the soldiers for **medevac**. She treated the two most seriously wounded soldiers first. Pvt. Brown remembered thinking, once the men were transported to safety, how quickly everything had happened. "I was the medic. It was my job to help them. I guess all of that stuff rushed into my brain and my muscles took over."

Thanks to Pvt. Brown's heroic actions, the two critically injured soldiers survived. On March 21, 2008, she received the Silver Star, the United States' third-highest medal given for bravery. She is the second female since World War II (1939–1945) to receive this medal.

More than 100 American female soldiers have died and more than 600 have been wounded in the conflicts in Iraq and Afghanistan.

Quick Thinking

Jason Mike

Rank:	Specialist (Later promoted to Sergeant)
Hometown:	Frankfort, Kentucky
Conflict:	Iraq War
Date:	March 20, 2005
Honor:	Silver Star

Quick thinking and bravery also made Spc. Jason Mike, a combat medic and member of the military police, a hero. On March 20, 2005, he was outside of Baghdad, Iraq, with his team. They were following a large convoy of about 30 trucks. Suddenly, 50 insurgents ambushed them. The enemy fighters fired from a nearby orchard.

A convoy of trucks in Iraq

The military police are part of the U.S. Army and provide support to soldiers during important missions.

As the convoy jolted to a stop, Spc. Mike's Humvee was sprayed with bullets. He and two fellow soldiers jumped out of the vehicle and returned fire. Moments later, the two soldiers were wounded. Spc. Mike reacted in an instant, dragging them under the truck for safety. Then he grabbed two guns, one in each hand, and began firing at insurgents in both directions. He continued to fire until the enemy finally backed off. When the ambush was over, he gave medical treatment to the injured soldiers.

For his heroic actions, Jason Mike (right) was awarded the Silver Star in June 2005. After receiving his award, he said, "I didn't go to Iraq to receive medals. I didn't go to be a hero. I went to do my job and do my part for my country in a time of need."

Fighting Through the Pain

Antony Gaston

Rank:	Specialist
Hometown:	Montclair, New Jersey
Conflict:	War in Afghanistan
Date:	May 29, 2011
Honor:	Purple Heart and Army Commendation Medal with Valor device

Often one of the hardest parts of a soldier's job is that he or she must continue on even after being seriously injured. Spc. Antony Gaston, an Army combat **engineer**, knows from experience what it means to fight through the pain. On May 29, 2011, during a **patrol** near Kandahar province, Afghanistan, insurgents attacked Spc. Gaston and his team. Spc. Gaston was struck in the leg by a golf ball-size piece of shrapnel. Horrible pain shot through his entire body.

Army soldiers on patrol

"The first thing I thought was 'They just shot at me; I need to shoot back,'" Spc. Gaston said. Despite his terrible injury, Spc. Gaston found the strength to get back on his feet and fire at the enemy. He continued to fire, knowing that the lives of his fellow soldiers were on the line. With Spc. Gaston's help, his team eventually forced the enemy to retreat. "Everything you ever go through makes you that much stronger for the next challenge that comes ahead," he said.

Combat engineers are trained soldiers, but they also have other special skills. For example, their job may include building bridges or roads, or finding and clearing IEDs from the battlefield.

A Purple Heart medal

On June 14, 2011, Antony Gaston received two honors: a Purple Heart and an Army Commendation Medal with Valor device. The Purple Heart is awarded to soldiers who are wounded or killed in battle. The Army Commendation Medal with Valor device is presented to soldiers who act heroically and show bravery when fighting an enemy.

A Job Like No Other

The men and women of the U.S. Army serve their country every day with **valor**. When asked to do the impossible, Army soldiers don't hesitate to act. Together, they charge through gunfire and bomb blasts to protect the United States and to save the lives of others.

Each soldier in the Army is trained to carry out a specific job, but by working as a team they are able to carry out their missions.

Medal of Honor winner Sgt. Giunta knows firsthand that being a good soldier means being part of a team. "If I am a hero," Sgt. Giunta has said, "then every man who stands around me, every woman in the military, every person who defends this country is."

There are more than 400,000 soldiers in the U.S. Army.

More Army Heroes

Here are a few U.S. Army soldiers who have performed heroic acts away from the front lines of war.

⭐ Sergeant First Class Tata Aga ⭐

On September 29, 2009, a **tsunami** struck the island of Tutuila in American Samoa in the South Pacific Ocean. The waves tore through Sgt. First Class Tata Aga's home, destroying it. "I won't forget that day; I had never seen something like that before," remembered Sgt. Aga. After the tsunami hit, he searched through the debris and found his U.S. Army uniform. He put it on and raced to help people in nearby villages. In the following days, he and other Army soldiers helped bring much-needed food and medical supplies to victims of the disaster. Sgt. Aga and 49 other Army soldiers received Humanitarian Service Medal awards for their work following the disaster.

A village on the island of Tutuila that was destroyed by the 2009 tsunami

★ Major Marci Hodge ★

Major Marci Hodge and a team of American troops worked with the local government in the city of Iskandariyah to get an Iraqi power plant up and running. She and her team employed at least 1,000 Iraqis to work at the plant. "People matter regardless of where they are," said Major Hodge. "It's your duty to give back." One of Major Hodge's other successes was to organize the shipment of thousands of children's books from Jordan, a country in the Middle East, to schools in Iraq. Major Marci Hodge was awarded the Bronze Star for helping the Iraqi people build a better future.

A Bronze Star

★ William White ★

A retired Army veteran, William White, is the founder and director of Camp Hope. White set up the camp to honor his son, a Marine killed in Iraq in 2006. The 180-acre (72-hectares) camp is located near St. Louis, Missouri. It's a place where injured members of the military and veterans can hunt, fish, and simply enjoy the outdoors. "This place is the best medicine," said Captain Joe Bogart, an Army combat engineer who was hit by an IED and lost an eye in Iraq in 2006. White said, "My initial thing was to help them learn to work with what they had. I had no idea it would be a healing process for them." In 2010, White was named Humanitarian of the Year by a group called American Veterans (AMVETS).

William White (left) talks to Captain Joe Bogart at Camp Hope.

Glossary

allies (AL-eyes) friends or supporters

Al Qaeda (AHL KAY-duh) the terrorist group that was responsible for the September 11 attacks on the United States

ambushed (AM-busht) attacked suddenly by surprise

Army Ranger (AR-mee RAYN-jur) a member of the U.S. Army who has been specially trained for difficult missions

base (BAYSS) the place soldiers live in and operate from

body armor (BOD-ee AR-mur) a special covering that is worn to protect a person in battle from gunfire and explosives

combat (KOM-bat) fighting between people or armies

convoy (KON-voi) a group of military vehicles traveling together for safety

engineer (en-juh-NIHR) a person who is trained to design or build things such as bridges, roads, or buildings

front lines (FRUHNT LINEZ) areas where battles take place

grenade (gruh-NAYD) a small bomb that is usually thrown by hand

hijacked (HYE-jackt) took control of by force

insurgents (in-SUR-juhnts) people who fight against a lawful government or lawful leaders

medevac (MED-uh-vak) the transportation of an injured person in a helicopter or airplane to a hospital

medic (MED-ik) someone trained to give medical care

mission (MISH-uhn) an important job

nuclear (NOO-klee-ur) having to do with a dangerous type of energy that produces radiation

patrol (puh-TROHL) to watch or travel around an area to protect it

Pentagon (PEN-tuh-gon) the five-sided building in Virginia that serves as the headquarters of the U.S. Department of Defense

platoon (pluh-TOON) a group of soldiers who train, work, and live together

prosthetic (pross-THET-ik) an artificial device that replaces a missing body part

province (PROV-uhnss) a district or region

raid (RAYD) a sudden surprise attack

retreat (ri-TREET) to move away or withdraw from a dangerous situation

sacrifice (SAK-ruh-fisse) to give up something important for a good reason

shrapnel (SHRAP-nuhl) pieces of metal from an exploded bomb or other device

Taliban (TAL-uh-ban) a military and political group that ruled Afghanistan from 1996 to 2001 and remains a strong force in the country

terrain (tuh-RAYN) a type of ground or land

terrorist group (TER-ur-ist GROOP) people who use violence and threats to get what they want

tsunami (tsoo-NAH-mee) a huge wave or group of waves caused by an underwater earthquake or volcano

unit (YOO-nit) a person, thing, or group that is part of a larger group

valor (VAL-ur) courage and bravery shown in battle

Bibliography

"Army Ranger Receives Medal of Honor for Afghanistan Heroics." CNN Politics. (July 12, 2011). www.cnn.com/2011/POLITICS/07/12/medal.of.honor/index.html?&hpt=hp_c2

www.army.mil/medalofhonor/giunta/

www.goarmy.com/about.html

Read More

Benson, Michael. *The U.S. Army (U.S. Armed Forces)*. Minneapolis, MN: Lerner Publications (2004).

Goldish, Meish. *Army: Civilian to Soldier (Becoming a Soldier)*. New York: Bearport Publishing (2011).

Griffin Llanas, Sheila. *Women of the U.S. Army: Pushing Limits*. Mankato, MN: Capstone Press (2011).

Learn More Online

To learn more about today's Army heroes, visit
www.bearportpublishing.com/ActsofCourage

Index

Afghanistan 4–5, 6, 9, 10–11, 14, 16, 18–19, 21, 24
Al Qaeda 4, 15
Army Ranger 6, 9

body armor 12
Brennan, Joshua 11, 13
Brown, Monica 18–19, 20–21

convoy 19, 22–23

engineer 24–25, 29

Gaston, Antony 24–25
Giunta, Salvatore 10–11, 12–13, 14, 27
grenades 6–7, 8, 12, 16

helicopters 6, 19
Humvees 19, 20, 23

improvised explosive device (IED) 19, 25, 29
insurgents 13, 14–15, 16, 19, 22–23, 24
Iraq 5, 21, 22–23, 29

Korengal Valley 5, 10

Medal of Honor 6, 9, 10, 13, 14, 17, 27
medevac 21
medic 18–19, 21, 22
Mike, Jason 22–23
military police 22
Miller, Robert J. 14–15, 16–17
missions 6, 12, 14, 18, 22, 26

Pashto 16
Pentagon 4
Petry, Leroy 6–7, 8–9, 10, 14
platoon 10, 12–13
prosthetic 9
Purple Heart 24–25

shrapnel 20, 24
Silver Star 18, 21, 22–23

Taliban 11, 15
terrorists 4–5, 6

weapons 5

About the Author

Joyce Markovics is a writer and editor in New York City. In writing this book, she wished to pay tribute to all the brave men and women who have risked their own safety for the sake of others.